Summer and W

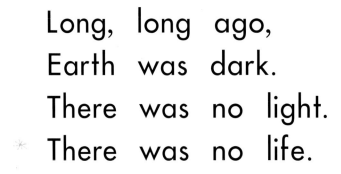

Long, long ago,
Earth was dark.
There was no light.
There was no life.

Yhi, the Sun,
was asleep.

2

Then, one day, Yhi woke up.
She opened her golden eyes.
She looked down at Earth.
It was dark. It was cold.

"I must wake Earth up,"
she said.

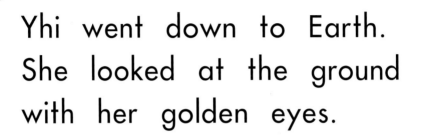

Yhi went down to Earth.
She looked at the ground
with her golden eyes.

Soon flowers grew,
grasses grew,
and trees grew.

Yhi looked at the mountains
with her golden eyes.

The ice melted.
The water ran down
the mountains.
It made rivers and lakes.

"Earth needs birds
and other animals," said Yhi.

So Yhi looked in dark places
with her golden eyes.
Birds and other animals
came out of the dark places
into her golden light.

Yhi looked at the flowers
and the trees. She looked
at the rivers and the lakes.
She looked at the birds
and the other animals.

"I must go back
into the sky now," she said.
"But I will make two seasons
so you will remember me."

"In summer, I will be near
and I will warm you.
In winter, I will be further away.
You will be cold
and some of you will sleep."

Then Yhi went up, up, up,
until she was just
a golden ball in the blue sky.

15

And she has stayed there ever since